MARAWI AND OTHER POEMS

Simeon Dumdum Jr.

Marawi & Other Poems
Marawi & Other Poems
Marawi & Other Poems
Marawi & Other Poems
Marawi & Other Poems

MARAWI & OTHER POEMS

Marawi & Other Poems
Marawi & Other Poems
Marawi & Other Poems
Marawi & Other Poems
Marawi & Other Poems

by Simeon Dumdum Jr.

by Simeon Dumdum Jr.

by Simeon Dumdum Jr.

by Simeon Dumdum Jr.

by Simeon Dumdum Jr.

BY SIMEON DUMDUM JR.

bughaw

by Simeon Dumdum Jr.

by Simeon Dumdum Jr.

by Simeon Dumdum Jr.

by Simeon Dumdum Jr.

by Simeon Dumdum Jr.

Published by Bughaw

Bughaw is an imprint of Ateneo de Manila University Press
Bellarmine Hall, ADMU Campus
Loyola Heights, Katipunan Avenue
Quezon City, Philippines
Tel.: (632) 426-59-84 / Fax (632) 426-59-09
E-mail: unipress@ateneo.edu
Website: www.ateneopress.org

Cover art by Marcel Antonio
Book design by Adonis Durado

The National Library of the Philippines CIP Data

Recommended entry:

Dumdum, Simeon, Jr.
Marawi and other poems / Simeon Dumdum, Jr. -- Quezon City :
Bughaw is an imprint of Ateneo de Manila University Press, [2019], c2019.
x, 68 pages ; 22.86 cm

ISBN 978-971-550-912-1

1. Filipino poetry. 2. Philippine poetry (English) I. Title.

899.2101 PR9550.6 P920190059

Acknowledgements: "Upon Seeing a Couple Kiss While I Am Taking Coffee Near the Airport" appeared in *Cordite Poetry Review* and "A Chance Encounter with Rodrigo Duterte in the Men's Room" in *Bloodlust: Philippine Protest Poetry from Marcos to Duterte* (Reyes Publishing, 2017).

For Jared Sebastian

Juliana Elise

and Francine Marie Genevieve

CONTENTS

A Chance Encounter with Rodrigo Duterte in the Men's Room 1
A Gloss on Rubens' *The Fall Of Man* 3
A Note on Susan's Photograph 4
A Rejoinder to T'ao Hung Ching's Answer 5
April 6
At John Steinbeck's House in Salinas, California 7
At the Lincoln Memorial 8
At the Moment 9
Beauty and the Beast 10
Ben & Jerry's Ice Cream Shop, Burlington, Vermont 11
Canzone for the New Year 12
Copla de Arte Mayor 15
Epistrophe 16
From Gingging and Me and the Monks from Eight Hundred Years Ago, by Way of Greeting You a Merry Christmas 17
I Wish I Had the Eyes of Emma Stone 18
In an Art Gallery in Columbus, Ohio 20
To Lady Gaga, While Listening to Her Sing Cole Porter's "Ev'ry Time We Say Goodbye" 21
Marawi 22
October 23
Ode to Joy 24
Of Names and the Marvelous 26
Outside a Starbucks Outlet at Paso Robles, California 27

Perhaps Tomorrow....28
Piero and the Resurrection....29
Salt and Light....32
September....36
The Gardener's Song....37
The Journey That Ends in Darkness Resumes in the Light....38
The Sound of One Hand Loving....40
The Universal Beauty of Seb Chua's Sculpture, "Under The Shades"....41
Time and Waiting....42
Times Square....43
Upon First Seeing the Grand Canyon....44
Upon Seeing a Couple Kiss While I Am Taking Coffee near the Airport....45
Wind-Blown Thought Balloons....46
Your Hair is a Cobweb of Light....47
A Toddler's Back-and-Forth from Light to Darkness....48
Chrysanthemums, Daisies, Carnations, and Peonies....49
Dear Emily....50
Dear Kobe....52
Duns Scotus and the Problem of Beauty....53
Hallelujah....54
How to Teach the Little Children All about the Resurrection....55
Julia and the Giraffe....56
Lai for Gingging on Her Birthday....58
Sestina for Easter Morning....59
Villanelle....61
Ode to the Red Moon....62
Serenade....63
Variation on the Second Law of Thermodynamics....64

A CHANCE ENCOUNTER WITH RODRIGO DUTERTE IN THE MEN'S ROOM

One day we met, Digong and I,
Which meeting was unusual,
For we were standing side by side
Before a men's urinal.

A conference he was attending
When fast he felt the need,
He left the hall and sought the toilet
Where shortly I had peed.

And on I stayed for the occasion
Finding it rare, this favor—
Standing beside a President
And with him passing water.

He glanced at me and I at him
With on my face a smile,
But he did not reciprocate,
I was just rank and file.

And it would not be presidential
To warm to anyone
He meets by chance in the men's room,
Who might just have begun.

The thing was just to do one's business
Of body or the state,
And having done with it just leave
That which remains to fate.

They say that he killed criminals
Or ordered their arrest
If they would not put up a fight,
Of this he would but jest.

But here at this latrine I relish
The opportunity
To have with such as presidents
A shared humanity.

A GLOSS ON RUBENS' *THE FALL OF MAN*

Rubens' *The Fall of Man* has just few flowers.
There's fruit, a bird and leaves, being a garden,
But not one rose? Is this really Eden
Where every bloom nods to the evening showers?
Perhaps a minor lapse in Rubens' powers?
And is this for a girl from kindergarten
To change, with a child's freedom in the bargain?
For there she is, now drawing on all fours.

Really, that Rubens thing's just my wild notion.
For sure, the child's hands shake (she is no angel),
But how do you expect her to compose?
Her lines crawl (no hint here of the Temptation),
And if to draw this mess is what she's able,
There is no such thing as a perfect rose.

A NOTE ON SUSAN'S PHOTOGRAPH

A single yellow shoe, high-heeled, lies on
Its side upon the sand near the sea's edge.
I guess it speaks of that which couples pledge
And break, this photograph taken by Susan
In Subic—other than a marathon
That left the shoe behind slumped on the sludge,
She could have run when he began to hedge
As talk moved on to marriage and beyond.
I'm not a fictionist—still, all these stories,
At bottom, bear on how the shoe had fallen
And earned being abandoned as a habit.
The waves themselves ignore it in their sorties,
And, from the way its shadow starts to lengthen,
Even the sun is all but set to leave it.

A REJOINDER TO T'AO HUNG CHING'S ANSWER

In Reply to the Emperor's Inquiry

'Among the hills what have you?'

'Among the hills, what have I?'
On the ridges there are many white clouds;
But these are only for my enjoyment–
They cannot be caught and passed on to your Majesty.

T'ao Hung Ching

Thank you for the reminder, T'ao Hung Ching,
Thank you, now that my mind is clear of clouds
And the day promises no chance of rain,
Although from the coolness around my ears
The ghost of it might now be falling somewhere.
Oh no there is nothing I can buy here,
Although I'm in a mall (not on a hill)–
They just don't have the item that I need,
And really I don't care for practical things
And would as soon look for a feathery cirrus
As a new faucet that the plumber needs.
Anything shaped like a feather brings joy.
There was a time the wife brushed my ear with
The down of a young duck while I was sleeping.
It felt like the tickle of whispered wisdom
And did not vex as much as made me smile,
Which may explain why now I feel enlightened
Each time I see the plumage of a cloud,
And hills are there for me to understand,
To wait for migratory clouds to pass
And drop like mail their messages of rain.

APRIL

I laid the cuttings yesterday
In a birdbath filled with rain.
When I checked them this morning,
They drifted towards me, offering
Their seven yellow flowers
And one little yellow bud.
All they had were leaves
When my mother's help
Nipped them off their stems
As though vegetables for the kitchen,
And wrapped them with paper
For our long trip home.
What was it in the night
That delighted and urged them
Into hasty flowering
Without waiting for the touch
Of earth and sun?
What was it in the night
And my sleep that made me wake up
This morning full of joy?

AT JOHN STEINBECK'S HOUSE IN SALINAS, CALIFORNIA

John Steinbeck, at the doorsteps of your old house are purple flowers.
The wife feels that we should have a photograph with this background.
Though hunger makes me impatient, love is stronger than hunger.

That hunger is not for food as much as art and its relics:
The bedroom where you were born, living spaces, dining area,
Where your mind must have made you eat with a side dish of stories,

Where we have broccoli cream, Philly cheese steak and Steinbeck tea–
A mixture of raspberry and I forget what other thing–
Which could be imagination, that growing in Salinas.

I pray, John, that I might have something like it, a glowing mind,
Such as yours, which flourishes with both fervor and compassion,
Which somehow I see in the flowers, and which will stay when they're gone.

AT THE LINCOLN MEMORIAL

This must be the true north
Of American politics, democracy's narcissus,
The stretch of ground from the Lincoln Memorial
Through the Washington Monument to the Capitol,
Which must needs point to itself then,
But does not twirl about like the compass
In the Arctic, which task pertains to the frisky
Breeze from the Potomac that this day
Keeps whirling around the Lincoln Memorial,
And which, as my wife and I position ourselves
Beside the reflection pool for a photograph,
Before our guide could click the camera,
Blows off her hat and sends it rolling
To join its image in the water.

AT THE MOMENT

The transmission lines
Have turned the full moon into
A two-string guitar

BEAUTY AND THE BEAST

They say there is a beast in every story,
But that's because we hunger for a tale.
We choose our days as measured on the scale
Of high adventure, think of history
As allegorical, and see in beauty
A village girl holding a book and pail,
Fated to find in hideousness a veil
Disguising both her hunter and her quarry.

The ending is a more than courteous dance.
The heart's an eye, the eye a heart that's blind.
That love's so fearful is known through the ages,
The story that appears when, by pure chance,
You stray into a library, and find
A book, and blow the dust off from its pages.

BEN & JERRY'S ICE CREAM SHOP, BURLINGTON, VERMONT

Ben & Jerry's offered Bob Marley's One Love,
Which I tried and reckoned too sweet an ice cream
For my health (but maybe the thoughts I had were nothing but sour grapes).

From the ice cream parlor, I made my way down,
Aided by a hand rail to steady my steps,
Otherwise unerring except for time's allowance of lost youth.

Midway through, pink roses enrobed the hand rail,
Leaving me with nothing to hold—I let go,
Charging it to fate, this abandonment to beauty come what may.

CANZONE FOR THE NEW YEAR

Another year, and so it starts again,
This back and forth of customary time.
Even the rains (must be a storm again,
But still too far to make landfall again).
How do we mark beginnings with all this
If the tail end is where we start again?
We seem to go through the same doors again
Although we have moved to another place,
But somehow the old doors got back in place.
So we can tell the same stories again?
As though in quest of a befitting ending
To life, which seems to end without an ending?

The last month of the calendar is ending.
Turn the remaining page over again
And draw the curtain, find the window ending
With light, which may not be part of the ending,
Which we ask for to pay for borrowed time,
Time beginning with you and with me ending,
A tale which just might have a happy ending,
And there may be no other tale than this,
One end of which each of us holds, of this
And that, to tie together as an ending,
And then to find ourselves in the same place,
Where everything (or nothing) will take place.

If that which lies ahead is the same place
Then we are left without a sort of ending.
But where roads disappear is one more place

That needs exploring, if it is the place
The map has shown again and yet again.
The calendar's a map whose proper place
Is in the clock, landscape that finds a place
Where it can serve the purposes of time,
Together with oblivion, which heals time,
Which needs rest and refreshment and a place
After the passage of a year like this,
And the survival of a life like this.

For we have seen lack and abundance, this
Is true, the sun and rain have kept our place
Sprouting with life, and we're grateful for this.
Nothing has veiled a sunrise such as this
Except the thought of night, of the day ending,
Month yields to month, that year yields to this,
Green of the fields to brown and green, and this
Is what's outside. And here inside? Again
The highs and lows of passion, and again
The promise one to the other that this
Arriving year will be another time
To make amends, dear Lord, just one more time.

Just one more time, O Lord, one more time.
We ask for nothing else, no more than this—
To step into that river one more time
And be forgiven, for there is no time
To lose, we have danced all over the place
To human music, to the lure of time
(Hip sways, that of the hourglass bleeding time),
Moving on the dance floor toward an ending,
Pushed to the New Year by an old year ending.

The river glows at dawn, sleep breaks, and time
Pulls light to dance in the valley again,
To call us back to life, and light, again.

So we begin another year again,
Uncertain and assured at the same time,
And keeping faith, and praying just for this—
A deeper happiness, a higher place
Where we can live our stories without ending.

COPLA DE ARTE MAYOR

With her, there were no clear excuses, and so
He joined her for coffee, and moved them away–
The things that would hide what they wanted to say
(The vase of tall flowers, the books, they must go)–
And then they began the same afternoon show,
The same conversation, whose drift would remain
The same, like the music they played, like the rain
That fell as they talked, and sought never to know.

EPISTROPHE

And of the sea, world of things reappearing,
I keep a watch, as terns keep reappearing
Every September, when the reappearing
Monsoon hastens the buds' reappearing.
Voyagers, will they be reappearing?
Somewhere the fading ships are reappearing
And at the quays the long lost, reappearing,
Hug the longed for, their dreamt day reappearing.
And here I wait for you, your reappearing
Told by the sea, which finds me reappearing
To see the drifting moment reappearing
After the waves, like a boat reappearing.

FROM GINGGING AND ME AND THE MONKS FROM EIGHT HUNDRED YEARS AGO, BY WAY OF GREETING YOU A MERRY CHRISTMAS

We send this poem as our Christmas card.
We could not find one suitable for you,
Knowing your predilection for the new
And fresh, whatever catches one off guard
And makes one smile, whatever is absurd,
Of which there are only a precious few,
The reason why it stays on our to-do
List, which we have decided to discard.

We have just seen a Star Wars episode
Shot on a rocky island, Skellig Michael.
There nothing's heard but waves and gulls at play,
Where once were monks who made it their abode.
For you we ask them for their prayer, a cable
Sent from a galaxy far, far away.

I WISH I HAD THE EYES OF EMMA STONE

I wish I had the eyes of Emma Stone
Now that the sun is out and I'm alone.
It's sunrise—every living thing perks up
For gifts, whatever light may offer, yup,
And here I am, all eyes on every dew
That glides down to the leaf tip, without you,
Who I'm sure would agree (if you were here)
That morning's newness would require a clear
Vision, new eyes, such as Proust has advised
For one to truly see and be surprised.

And noontime begs the use of the same premise
That eyes should be as wide and wise as Emma's
Because the heat will call up a mirage
And what I see may be a camouflage
Of the real—gardens for busy bus stations
(The buzz of bees for aimless conversations),
You hurrying instead of someone else.
And I could fall for these and other spells
If not for eyes that need no telescope
To know the land, its every bend and slope.

And why the eyes of Emma Stone? Because
Her eyes betray emotion without pause.
It can be wonder, joy, pain or betrayal,
The feeling just emerges, without trial,
In her eyes, forming like the dew on grass,

A cloud at first and then a watery mass.
Seeing means nothing if without remembrance,
If it cannot make out any resemblance
In me, a pianist playing a tone
Recalled by you, or such as Emma Stone.

IN AN ART GALLERY IN COLUMBUS, OHIO

As to art, its insistence is the bane of reality.
On High Street, place called Short North, in Columbus in Ohio,
As elsewhere, imagination trumps everything except fact.

Inside the art galleries, in one of which was a painting
Of a field full of flowers bent by the wind of midsummer,
Which was I, for nothing moved there but my eyes.

How could I, despite myself, not be wind-blown among the flowers,
And be part of the landscape inside the frame within this room,
Which dissolved and broke its borders when I approached to touch them?

The painting gave me license to get inside and back again,
Not the door, set next to it, as beautiful if not as real,
Across which was written a sign, which bore the words, "No entry."

TO LADY GAGA, WHILE LISTENING TO HER SING COLE PORTER'S "EV'RY TIME WE SAY GOODBYE"

Midnight finds us listening to you while packing.
There's no better way to wait for morning and the taxi.
There won't be goodbyes—we will travel, both of us,
And your voice, it leaves the lament of love behind,
Building distance separating night from morning.
Gaga, as you lean close to the pianist, his fingers,
I believe, could fumble and jazz up,
And, drawing music from passion,
Move from minor to major.

MARAWI

When they came, pounded their way through Marawi, waving black flags,
When they stormed a hospital and torched houses and emptied jails,
I was home many miles away, about to nap, book in hand.

When they sacked a cathedral and grabbed a priest and his people,
The day slipped into evening, promising rest
And stray talk in the balcony, where we would sit, watching stars.

We woke up to a morning of enough warmth and window light,
But by then folk were fleeing by the thousands
From their homes in the wrecked city, carrying all but nothing.

The women trapped in a school kept to the floor,
Holding on to the hijabs given by friends,
Their ears glued to the jihadists outside the rooms, passing by.

At that time, the wife and I were having snacks
In a place with a good view of the channel
Where the boats sailed to points south, to Mindanao, I surmised,

Where the thugs shot civilians with their hands tied
When they caught the poor people about to flee,
And shouting "Allahu Akbar" with every shot to the head,

Or cut head, and seeing this, a refugee
Sought escape across a stream only to drown,
At which time, we were in a mall cooling our heels, and our souls.

OCTOBER

Time to view, this October, Andrew Wyeth's "Wind from the Sea,"
His painting of a window through which the wind enters a room—
And my mind, a much deeper room, whose back walls are invisible.

Between me and the wide shore and the great sea (on the left side),
A curtain, tattered and thin, streams with the wind which blows it in—
All the proof that a spirit gives, though too briefly, of its path?

I don't know—the curtain seems a ragged veil a dancer left,
Which is all that her suitor, the hopeless wind, has in its clutch,
To tense up, in her memory, with excitement and desire.

ODE TO JOY

Joy, you are a little crazy.
Once I woke up to the clipclop
Of a horse outside the window.
Was it ghostly? Oh yes, of course,
But I smiled, elated just to
Hear the sound of hooves which seemed to
Exit sleep to join the morning.
Just like that you come to me.
Joy, you visit like the dew–
Fragile sparkle, beautiful,
Happening when nothing's happening,
Such as at McDonald's yesterday
When I chanced upon a couple
Sitting near a window shadowed
By the afternoon's decline.
I just found the sight so blissfull
That my coffee and filet-o-fish
Lost their heat as I reflected
On the silence which had bound them
Like a wedding cord and veil.

Schiller says you come from the
Womb of the Elysian Fields
(Wombs I know, I think, but not the
Other named, wherever that is),
Being that which justifies
Love between a man and woman,
Love that makes us all God's children,
Watched and blessed by a drift of stars.
Thanks, Herr Schiller, as to van Dyke

("Joyful, joyful, we adore Thee")
You are what makes worship worship,
Turning us toward that Rising,
Opening to the east like flowers.

OF NAMES AND THE MARVELOUS

Quickly I gave the name,
That of the baby which
We were godparents of,
Not knowing that the priest
Really meant the infant
That came before our own.
Without delay, the priest
Baptized the little one,
And so soon it was over.
And they were at a loss,
The parents, who just stared
In silence at each other,
Because their baby now
Carried a stranger's name.
Still they accepted it,
Believing that the name
Could only come from God,
Which for me stands to reason,
For He alone can name,
Who is Unnameable.

OUTSIDE A STARBUCKS OUTLET AT PASO ROBLES, CALIFORNIA

The orange roses
Why is it that I love them
When they don't love me

PERHAPS TOMORROW

Always there are promises waiting outside.
Daybreak has the tendency to disturb sleep,
And the eyes that open expand the windows onto the bright land,

And we see that everything has its own time,
Gathers light and shape and then rolls like dewdrop,
Flaming up while falling (and blossoming inside, an unseen bud).

So we settle into our own desired rest,
Mornings when dreams start to arrive like wild geese
In September—hopes that may find a roost, tomorrow, if not now.

PIERO AND THE RESURRECTION

What thoughts did Piero della Francesca have
When he painted the fresco of the Resurrection?
Was it a bright day in Sansepolcro
As he applied the pigments on the lime and sand?
Anyway, the real brush is the mind,
The light can slant to put the hand
In shadow, but the mind remains on fire.
Piero was a mathematician, and knew that,
In his case, numbers escape
And disguise themselves as colors,
Especially at dawn, when half-asleep the eyes
Let go of the reckonings of grief,
Although there were claims by Vasari
That Piero had gone blind in old age,
Which is sad, because life is nothing
But light to a painter.
In fact, this afternoon has been too full of dazzle
To last, and the misgivings
About the coming night are fading
In the west, way beyond the islands,
Whose ghosts visit our gaze every morning.
The world has the tenderness of fruit
About to fall, which, with his brush, the artist
Must be ready to capture at any time,
Hoping that it stays in the air long enough
To stretch the moment's brightness to its limits,
Much like a dewdrop rolling down a leaf,
Holding out for as long as it can to gather into itself
All that it wishes us to remember.

And so what does Piero della Francesca
Want me to keep in mind
As I gaze at his fresco of the Resurrection?
I see the risen Christ about to step out
Of a sarcophagus, a foot set forward,
Like an athlete before a race, his right hand
Holding the banner of victory.
Death breaks the mirror into fragments,
Which by ourselves we cannot put together,
But we are promised a light that will reveal
All of the world whose view we have lost,
A dawn in which as yet time seesaws
Between growth and decline.
And time is not just you and me together
In a coffee shop, watching the ships
Hurrying west towards sunset, while to the south,
Blazing with the last rays of the day,
White herons fly their last journey before dark,
And couples wait by the sea
Like candles melting with desire.
The wait can be a sleep in each other's arms,
Or a sleep induced when time faces
The eternity that perhaps it fails
To understand, which might be the sleep
Of the guards below the sarcophagus
(One of them being Piero himself,
The one whom Christ's staff touches.)
By the way, how fitting that the fresco should lead
To the hall of judges, who prayed
Before the painting as they entered,
Such that, as someone mentioned,
The fresco of the Resurrection "protects the judge
And purifies the judged," not to mention that
The judge himself needs purifying.

As can happen, the sunlight that enters his courtroom,
Because of the arrangement of the interior,
May not reach the inside of his chambers.

There's nothing that blows my mind
More than the Resurrection of Christ,
Which makes every painting on the subject
Deserving of Aldous Huxley's comment
On Piero della Francesca's work,
"It stands before us in entire
And actual splendor, the greatest picture
In the world."
Perhaps, what makes it so
Is its power to make us see with eyes closed,
As though in prayer, which is a kind of sleep
That is awake, a death that is alive,
In which every noise is a song,
Every word a soft mention of one's name,
And every look a vision of a world in which
Everything flies.

SALT AND LIGHT

Our hands, as well as eyes,
Meet when you pass the salt.
Indeed, life is encounter
(Buber has it down pat).
I could have asked you for
Your name, but you're my wife,
My cure-all, like salt-water,
Sweat, tears or the sea, as
Isak Dinesen said.
I'd go to war for you
As people did for salt,
Which set off great upheavals.
At least no one has asked
That I pay for your smile.
This would be like a tax
On salt, one of the fuses
Of the French Revolution,
And which made Gandhi lead
The people to the sea
On a march towards freedom.
And yet no salt, whose weight
Was worth in gold, has value
More than you—caravans
Traversing the desert,
Carrying salt pillars,
The Roman wagons wheeling
Down the Via Salaria
Direct from the salt flats
By the Tyrrhenian Sea,
I would have joined them all

If I had you beside me,
Or would have forgone each
Finding myself alone.
The real salt is love,
Kindness, the glass of water
Offered to one unknown,
Which need can turn one into
To him who has a heart
That's curved upon itself,
As mine becomes at times.
May my hand turn to salt,
Which once was currency,
My words be caravans
On the salt road to you,
Or to the stranger who
May have your face, an angel
I might have entertained
Without my knowing it
By being welcoming,
As you are to me now
Handing me the salt shaker.

The evening's getting darker,
And, as you show me how
To light the lamp you're keeping
For years inside a garret,
The thoughts I have detained
Fly out towards a spindle,
Which turns the white moths into
Light threads that blunder through
Your fingers like fire ribbons.
I sense your hesitancy,
As though eyeing a fault
Somewhere, while your hand mimes

The flame. Near a bookshelf
You set the lamp apart
To have a wider view
Of that to which we're thrown—
The space which things that quiver
Now wish to be free of,
Released from flesh and bone,
To take off beyond reach
For light's unending sea.
The shadows on the wall,
They're all for you and me
Just mere shadows of slats
Inside a lighted area,
Which leave us deeply burning
To be eternal dwellers
Within light's Nessus' shirt,
Love, the pure relevance.
What I can do with you
Tonight is contemplate
The light as diadem
Of the lamp next to me,
Which is beyond the need
Of but an earthly notion.
Before the light, one uses
None other than love's syntax,
If only for a while,
And always one is tasked
With turning all reversals
With kindness as default.
The arm I put around you
Is light's arm—what light said
Is the word that's between us,
A word that does not waver
Because it is our life,

And there is nothing better.
What we are looking at
When we lose light's favor
Are shadows, but we're called
Not to the night, but sunrise.

SEPTEMBER

Of course, it could just be the light of rain,
And in the drizzle there may be departures.
Perhaps we know nothing of them, the pain
Of those who stay, who themselves have adventures
In just remaining, fighting off such creatures
As pet despairs, the emptiness of light,
Blunder of moth wings on September nights.

THE GARDENER'S SONG

Go, my garden of flowers,
Do not wither yet, or worse,
Be bare before tomorrow's
Blind arrow hits the right rose.
Do keep them fresh, the dahlias,
For the soft sound of her yes.
The birds that sing the questions
Have notions to chirp my chance.
All I ask for of gardens
Is trick the time into dance,
So she'll wait for me also—
With my shadow, garden, go!

THE JOURNEY THAT ENDS IN DARKNESS RESUMES IN THE LIGHT

The way waves inwardly,
Hangs weightless, vanishes.
The heat keeps things hazy
And the hurt uncertain.
Still, joy is the journey
Of nothing, just distance,
Waiting, and wakefulness,
All without insistence.
Lilies shake the landscape
As I laugh at sunrise,
Like bells blessed by crosswinds
Birds sway on their perches.
Mind's midsummer gushes
At the morning glory,
Sky-colored and shining,
Stalk dripping with rainfall.
Days veined with vermillion
And touched with hushed voices
Deck our destination
With desire's finery.
Is it home we hope for,
Having reached the evening?
Light is the lark's arrow
That leaps into nothing.
For to stay with stories
Is to turn from searching

And tie time's persistence
To an easy heartbeat.
No road runs endlessly
But must rest in darkness,
No door dreams unshuttered
But must dress for morning.

THE SOUND OF ONE HAND LOVING

I have no choice but make do with my left
Since I have lost the use of my right hand,
Which has become cold to motion and heft–
My "frozen shoulder," a term used offhand,
Has made my left hand busy without end.
Which is why now I feel being cared for,
Bathed, fed and cuddled, by a one-armed
lover.

THE UNIVERSAL BEAUTY OF SEB CHUA'S SCULPTURE, "UNDER THE SHADES"

Sitting on the ground, she upraises one knee
To support her infant, who rests on her arm.
She appears exhausted, but grateful for a sapling to lean on.

Probably the tree is too short to give shade,
But it has shade-giving within its young soul,
And though she's small, a mother's love's wider than the shade of a huge tree.

She is faceless, but this is just for art's sake,
For we know where mothers belong, their real class
Being beauty itself, and not the beautiful, which does not last.

TIME AND WAITING

When you left, the sun
Assumed your foot—your sandal
Became a sundial.

TIMES SQUARE

What we told each other on reaching Times Square
I would have remembered if they had not come
Speaking all at once, overjoyed to find us already in New York.

At Carmine's, baked clams, and of course the big laughs
Exing years of separation from loved ones,
Winters that we, visitors, could not have imagined that July day.

Then along pedestrian plaza, we met
Someone holding up a sign saying "Free Hugs."
Quickly you held on to your hat although there clearly was no wind,

Not in Times Square where we had only ourselves
And reached for each other as in a swift flood,
Then embraced, attempting to stop the countdown to the ball drop.

UPON FIRST SEEING THE GRAND CANYON

I did not expect that the view would hit me
From inside, exploding in silence—first times
Always have a freshness that surprises by making the unseen seen.

Was it not the marvelous I could make out
In the vastness spreading outwards inside me,
Urging me to prayer, without whose sights I struggle to see far?

At a deer, for instance, while coming downhill
By a forest, just an odd glance, a quick glimpse,
Then it disappeared, for the bus, behind time, hastened to move on.

UPON SEEING A COUPLE KISS WHILE I AM TAKING COFFEE NEAR THE AIRPORT

What if no one winessed the couple's quick kiss?
What if I was not in the coffee shop now,
Having cappuccino alone and gazing at those who pass by?

Coincidences mark the imprint of this hour.
Whether they be casual or one of great weight,
How could I tell? Only the kissers knew the import of their kiss.

Kisses I have known (and among them were yours,
I recall one when we were going upstairs,
That's another story, however youthful, honest, a pure joy –

As I think all kisses must be if done here,
At a coffee shop just beside the airport).
Well, to them, the kissers, I raise this cup of coffee and my heart.

WIND-BLOWN THOUGHT BALLOONS

Wild balloons, their strings with a compact square knot,
Straining, tugging furiously on their tied ends,
Try to lift their moorings, attempting to remove them from firm ground.

I can only laugh, for I know the odd wind
Is behind all this, the balloons are pure fools,
Thinking that their strength is their own—I made a similar faux pas

Years ago, when youth was the theme of my song,
Brash, inflated, drifting across the old earth,
Blue balloon turning in the dark and kept afloat by a true light.

YOUR HAIR IS A COBWEB OF LIGHT

(A birthday poem for Gingging)

How can any wanderer miss this bright thread
Hung above the path in the midst of your trees?
May it be a filament ripped from sunshine spreading around you?

Or is it a blessing, a strand of clear grace,
True surprise, so sudden, a real and free gift,
Dew that stretches all the way to a thinness almost beyond sight?

There's a spider spinning a web of pure light
That awaits my passage and then it gives way,
Gossamer that feels like a strand of your hair falling on my face.

A TODDLER'S BACK-AND-FORTH FROM LIGHT TO DARKNESS

Already she could understand
If spoken to, such words as dog
And cat, said with a bark and meow,
Draw out a smile of recognition
From her, age one year and a half.
And her vocabulary grew one morning
When I asked her to come down from
Her mother's lap and walk from shade
To sunlight, and, as she did this,
I said, "Shade," and then I said, "Sunlight,"
Pointing to wherever she was,
Which I think registered because
She would move from one to the other,
Depending on which I would mention,
Which of this book's, the day's two pages,
And when she was back in the sunlight,
I drew near and said to her, "Shadow,"
And made her look back to her shadow,
Which waved its arms as she waved hers,
And thereby I could see that somehow
They'd come to understand each other.
Light must have shadows to make sense.
Meaning's the shadow a word casts
Moving across a page of light,
Much like that which a toddler drags–
A small, dark blanket in the sunshine.

CHRYSANTHEMUMS, DAISIES, CARNATIONS, AND PEONIES

Chrysanthemums, daisies, carnations, and peonies—
The flowers in airy verandas where once more
I saw you, but you did not notice me pass
Because an incautious balloon had got snagged
In one of the branches that stretched towards you,
Which popped and alarmed the two pigeons below,
And then you saw me and you asked for my name,
Which I could not give since a wind blew across
And lifted my hat, which it sent to the back,
And after I got it you had disappeared
Inside the big house with its airy verandas,
Chrysanthemums, daisies, carnations, and peonies.

DEAR EMILY

I write like this because,
Having reread your poems,
I wonder how it would be
To roam around your rooms.

I could have gone to Amherst,
About two and a half hours
From Roosevelt Hotel in Manhattan,
Instead of New York's towers.

I could have seen eternity
From your upstairs window
This summer, this day in July—
Eternity is the sky's innuendo.

And there's your writing desk.
Can I get a chair, Emily,
And sit across from you?
Do you have tea?

I want to ask you something.
No, not about the dashes
(Which I use too) or how
You write and do the dishes.

I want to ask about faith
And disbelief and love and loss
And how with just a stanza
You put it all across.

Since you could taste eternity,
There's nothing you can't bite.
The truth is on the tip of every tongue
You only need to say it.

Do you not trim that tongue
With these scissors, the quatrain,
And at the same time trim the wick
Of the lamp of your brain?

If people hardly see you,
I know why, I myself
Who sit across from you
Might as well face an empty shelf.

Because you're in eternity,
And I am not before you.
I'm in New York, in Times Square,
And will be gone in a day or two.

I'll be going home
After a stay in San Francisco,
And view eternity
From an airplane window.

DEAR KOBE

Dear Kobe, I am writing from a country you have been to,
Perhaps twice, the Philippines (same area as California),
Still I know you won't get to read or know about this letter.

I did play some basketball as a young man, once in a while.
It was then that the Celtics dominated most every game,
And this guy, one Wilt Chamberlain, was the big star of the court.

Bill Russell, I understand, was no less great, a shot-blocker.
He rivalled Wilt Chamberlain in the rebounds, for the Celtics.
But Kobe, I am digressing, I'm not into basketball,

Not really, although I watched NBA games on occasion.
What I found in you, Kobe, was your passion for basketball.
More than skill, on the court you showed a ball of fire, you yourself,

Which was why, when off your hands, the ball flew with your own mind,
Which was why, without delay, it made a nest of the ring,
And its swoosh into the circle was a genuine reunion.

And for you, the turning earth, the "pale blue dot," was basketball,
Which you spun on a finger, whether half asleep or wide awake,
In the court of your consciousness, on whose surface life was played—

Basketball before the game, the dribbling that of the heart,
Basketball after the game, when what you held was your fatigue,
Which you were unable to toss, yourself being its basket.

That was then, now it's goodbye to basketball and the Lakers,
But is it? Because no one can say goodbye to one's own self,
And the ball will roll after you as your shadow, Yours—

DUNS SCOTUS AND THE PROBLEM OF BEAUTY

Duns Scotus looked out the window
At a garden of roses. It was midsummer.
A whiff of bonfires still hung in the air.
He saw clumps of the White Rose of York,
Which spoke to him of the Virgin Mary,
The Mystical Rose, and were as tall as he.
As well as the fragrant red Damask,
Which as he recalled was a residue
Of the Crusades, and then out of whimsy
He wished Thomas Aquinas was there
So he could ask him what he thought of the roses,
Scotus was sure that the Dominican would launch
Into a discussion of beauty and God.
Employing his usual method of question,
Counter statement and reply, to which
He would respond with his own notions.
Did infinite beauty mean, for instance,
An infinite number of roses, spreading
From the garden of the Franciscans in Oxfordshire,
Out towards London and the Hebrides,
Covering the earth and, let me add, the planets,
Upwards to the Milky Way, the galaxies
And beyond, spilling over the borders
Of time and space? Or could a single rose
Be infinitely beautiful, and have within itself
Perfect clarity, wholeness and balance,
In other words, the radiance that pulsates
From the boundless inner life of God?
And Scotus wondered if that rose had a thorn too
And if that thorn was infinite and capable
Of infinite pain.

HALLELUJAH

Lydia the hair dresser could not stop crying.
Her parrotlet Hallelujah was gone.
When she came home she found its cage half-open.
The door towards the roof-deck was ajar.
Was it the route of little Hallelujah?
She looked around for feathers, anxious that
A cat might have done to it what she feared.
But the breeze moved nothing except the curtain,
Which the four-odd-inch yellow Hallelujah
Would tug when Lydia let it roam around.
During her nap it would sleep in her hair.
It twiddled with the teaspoon in her beak
To stir her coffee while she had her breakfast.
She was in church when she thought of its name.
She put it in a box and through a hole
Kept saying to the young bird "Hallelujah,"
And soon it learned to flap its wings in answer
And did the same when Lydia clapped her hands.
She put it in its cage before she left
After it had fed on sunflower seeds.
The cage door, now she recalled, was not hooked.
When all her efforts to find it had failed,
She went to church, prayed to Saint Anthony,
And was about to leave when of a sudden
She saw a flock of sparrows flying by
And followed them to where they might be hiding.
Old Father Paul smiled in the sacristy
When he heard someone from inside the church
Clapping her hands and shouting, "Hallelujah."

HOW TO TEACH THE LITTLE CHILDREN ALL ABOUT THE RESURRECTION

"Baby, do you love me?" the mother asked,
Tying the little girl's dress with a ribbon.
The three-year-old said, "Yes," her voice a whisper,
The way one speaks when truly meaning it,
Which pleased the mother so much that she wanted
To have her daughter say it one more time.
"I didn't hear you," she said, teasing her,
The daughter, not less meaning it, yelled, "Yes!"
At once she gained a tight embrace and kiss.

They were at Mass, that third Sunday of Easter.
They occupied a pew in front, right side.
During the Gospel reading, the child asked
For milk—her mother offered her the bottle.
The priest capped his homily with this question,
"Do you believe that Christ rose from the dead?"
All he heard was a mutter of assent,
Which the churchgoers made under their breath,
Which was too weak to signify conviction,
And this the priest had sensed, and now he forced
The issue, roaring, "I did not hear you!"
And then a voice was heard, which made the priest
And congregation turn towards the side
In the direction of a feeding bottle.

JULIA AND THE GIRAFFE

Little Julia was close to tears.
She didn't want her father to
Take her into his arms and lift
Her up towards the stalled giraffe,
But there was just no other way,
He thought, while elevating her.
A while back, they watched a cheetah,
Which would not look at her no matter
How much she pressed her face against
The glass wall, prompting little Julia
To seek her dad with a sad face.
Before that they drove through a field
In a safari car—they passed
By zebras, antelopes, gazelles.
Julia had wanted to join them
But the car would not stop; besides,
They were not allowed to get down.
They skipped the crocodiles and went
Straight to the more friendly giraffes.
On the way, the father put Julia
On a dwarf horse, on which she bounced
To make it run, but it kept still.
And there they were, standing before
The two giraffes, which were fenced off.
Still they could hold their necks beyond
The fence and be fed by the crowd
With bits of apples stuck on sticks,
Which sold for fifty pesos each.
Julia embraced her father's leg,
Her way of asking for a stick,
Which she got, and the two-year-old

Immediately raised the stick up,
Tiptoeing as much as she could,
But she was just too small and short.
The giraffe could not get the apple
With its now overly stretched tongue,
Which, while its tip could touch the fruit,
Could not completely curl around it
To flip it up into the mouth.
I understood the child's frustration
As well as what her father did.
Time would see Julia grow tall, but
A giraffe's hunger could not wait.

LAI FOR GINGGING ON HER BIRTHDAY

What's age anyway?
O the resumé
Might call
For such as birthday,
And yours is today
As well–

Birthdays are to view
New worlds to get to,
Like those
Where flowers outdo
Most each other to
A rose,

Which are really here,
And in truth as near
To us
As the thing we hear
Whispered to the ear,
As this–

Love's a fugitive
To catch and forgive
Anew,
A life to relive
Daily, and to give
To you.

SESTINA FOR EASTER MORNING

How completely confused is history.
To me it seems to keep clear of the answers,
Always like leaves blown away by the questions
Until they stop before the utmost riddle,
That baffling labyrinth, the whorl of time,
Which sheds its petals like the garden rose.

The thing I want to say is this—Christ rose
From the dead, therefore what can history
Say of this, what can that house owner, time,
Say to policemen who ask for the answers
To incidents within his house, the riddle
That clarifies and solves rather than questions?

I was about to ask you certain questions
When a wind blew from the west, the moon rose
Above the trees, and like an ancient riddle
The growing night fell in with history,
Which you remarked on by way of your answers
To what you called the enigma of time.

Someone played the piano at one time.
The music widened both our ears, like questions,
And its arpeggios offered all the answers
As bells above the waves that fell and rose.
Who was she, what was her history?
How could so clear a music be a riddle?

Life, than which there can be no greater riddle,
The beginning and end of it, which time
Unrolls and severs, in whose history,

Its sunsets and sunrises, live the questions,
Is what we have, the one mysterious rose
That seeks to grow towards the source of answers.

The growth of restlessness towards the answers,
The heart to put at rest the endless riddle
Of pain, of death, which the one who rose
From the dead has sought to redeem from time,
And then there will not be any more questions,
An angel to heal the wounds of history.

Reason and history might have the answers,
For some, but not all questions, like this riddle—
Time is the thorn, eternity the rose.

VILLANELLE

There is a lion prowling in the park.
You think your fear will vanish with the light?
It will remain there and grow with the dark.

If you will, take this as a wild remark.
But wait for that of which you will catch sight.
There is a lion prowling in the park.

Whenever it begins to stalk its mark,
A lion seeks the dusk, becomes the night.
It will remain there and grow with the dark.

If as yet nothing leaps in a wide arc
At you, think not that everything's all right.
There is a lion prowling in the park.

Its eyes are burning but they have no spark.
Among the trees, sunless because of height,
It will remain there and grow with the dark.

If you should meet it at last, do not fight
With your self, asking if it's all a lark.
There is a lion prowling in the park.
It will remain there and grow with the dark.

ODE TO THE RED MOON

Oh Red Moon, though very far, you're really near and reachable,
For the night will bare nothing we cannot touch with our wild eyes,
While our hands have come to behave with their blindness and silence.

When was it when we last saw a sight like you while together
When yourself had turned scarlet from earth's twisting and untwisting,
None of which was a recentness we remember when awake?

Oh Blood Moon, how we have gone into the night with just our thoughts
And seen you, an Autumn leaf, live as ember in the darkness,
Pulsing with the human season that has found life despite ours.

This I know—that we have known the night's reasons in your presence,
Why the stars quickly retreat and disappear to give you room
But briefly, before we return to the lamplight to retire.

SERENADE

When you smile I miss the road, I am lost
In worlds crossed and harrowed.
But a light and happy load
Is your love, true or borrowed.

I looked in front, but you were beyond me,
By the sea, a letter
Away, with nothing to care
But the changes of weather.

The waiting has made me grow all attuned
As wound and no arrow.
Tonight, if you're a no-show
I'll climb up to your window.

VARIATION ON THE SECOND LAW OF THERMODYNAMICS

Disturb an infant's sense of order
And you disturb the universe—
A precious lesson learned this evening.
Francine, our two-year-old granddaughter,
Has everything paired in her mind,
And this might well be set in stone.
She matches them, people and things
That look alike or correspond.
In her eyes, things are binaries.
The world's a set of ordered pairs.
For instance, birds evoke the sky
And always must stay there with rainbows.
Her grandma bought a dark brown hat
During a trip to Strawberry Farms
And wore it everywhere, and this
The little girl could not forget.
Unknown to her, her mother bought
A hat of the same make and color,
Such that, after I had installed a
Celestial globe on a center table
(I am a bit of a star freak),
And carried Francine in my arms,
She cried when she noticed her mother
Wearing a brown hat which she thought
Was stolen from her good grandmother,
And would not be appeased at all
Even when the lady appeared,
Wearing her hat from Strawberry Farms,

Which only worsened the situation,
Because the little girl felt cheated
And went wild, almost knocking off
The globe and stars from the small table.

BOOKS BY THE AUTHOR

Non-fiction

Love in the Time of the Camera
My Pledge of Love Cannot Be Broken
Ah, Wilderness

Poetry

The Gift of Sleep
Third World Opera
Poems Selected and New
If I Write You This Poem, Will You Make It Fly
To the Evening Star
Eighty-four Words for Sorrow
Partly Cloudy
Letter from Fatima
The Poet Learns to Dance, the Dancer Learns to Write a Poem
Aimless Walk, Faithful River